The Heart
of God

The Heart of God

Poems of Life | Prayers of Love

With a new foreword by Bashabi Fraser
and 25 Additional Poems *by the Author*

TUTTLE Publishing
Tokyo | Rutland, Vermont | Singapore

Published by Tuttle Publishing, an imprint of Periplus Editions (HK) Ltd.

www.tuttlepublishing.com

Expanded Edition Copyright © 2022 Periplus Editions (HK) LTD

The text on pages xx was taken from Indian Thought and Its Development, by Albert Schweitzer, copyright © 1936 by the Beacon Press.
The photograph on the frontispiece is by LLAMAS, Boston.

Library of Congress Control Number: 2022936146

ISBN 978-0-8048-5548-8

Distributed by

North America, Latin America & Europe
Tuttle Publishing
364 Innovation Drive
North Clarendon, VT 05759-9436 U.S.A.
Tel: 1 (802) 773-8930
Fax: 1 (802) 773-6993
info@tuttlepublishing.com
www.tuttlepublishing.com

Asia Pacific
Berkeley Books Pte. Ltd.
3 Kallang Sector #04-01
Singapore 349278
Tel: (65) 6741-2178
Fax: (65) 6741-2179
inquiries@periplus.com.sg
www.tuttlepublishing.com

25 24 23 22   10 9 8 7 6 5 4 3 2 1   2205VP
Printed in Malaysia

TUTTLE PUBLISHING® is a registered trademark of Tuttle Publishing, a division of Periplus Editions (HK) Ltd

Contents

Foreword

Leave out my name from the gift
if it be a burden,
but keep my song.
—*Fireflies*, No. 14

Rabindranath Tagore (1861–1941), the Indian writer, educator and environmentalist, was brought to the world's attention when he was awarded the Nobel Prize for Literature in November 1913, making the Prize truly international as he was the first non-Westerner to win it. It was a unique moment as Tagore's work—literary, educational and socio-economic—was celebrated by this recognition when he was still the subject of a subject nation. When Tagore received the Nobel, he was already a household word in his native Bengal and a much respected voice across India. Henceforth, he would simply be referred to as "the Poet" by many of his friends and contemporaries in letters, addresses and references to him.

Of his own upbringing Rabindranath[1] says, "I was born and brought up in an atmosphere of the confluence of three movements [religious, literary and social] all of which were revolu-

---

1. The members of the Tagore family were extremely talented and were renowned writers and artists, so in order to avoid confusion, I refer to Rabindranath Tagore by his first name in the Foreword. This is customary in Bengal as in all literary and critical references, Rabindranath Tagore is referred to as Rabindranath.

tionary."[2] (Tagore, "A Poet's School," p. 666). Rabindranath's entire body of work is signified by this confluence, a meeting of cultures, philosophies and ideas from the East and West. The "revolutionary" encapsulates the transformational and modern nature of his own creative output (and that of his family members), which remains relevant and resonates with all that is precious and needs protection in humanity. Rabindranath Tagore, embodies the Universal Man.

At Jorasanko, the home of the Tagores in Calcutta (now Kolkata), popularly known as Thakurbari, Tagore experienced a hub of creative consciousness and flowering, where the family members were immersed in a whirlwind of activities that was reflective of traditional forms and open to adopting and sustaining influences from abroad. This is the core from which Tagore's thoughts and work, his wishes and prayers for his country and the world, sprang.

The Poet was a polymath, a novelist, a short story writer, a playwright, an autobiographer, a letter writer, an essayist, a lyricist, a composer (having written over 2,200 songs), a children's writer, an artist (with over 2,000 paintings), a sermon and travel writer. He was also a performing artist—a singer of his own songs, a reciter of his own poems and a performer in his own plays and dance dramas. He was an artistic innovator who created his distinctive brand of songs (Rabindrasangeet) and his own form of dance (the expressive Rabindranritya), which have allowed professionals to specialize in these forms to this day.

---

2. Rabindranath Tagore, "To the Public at the Theatre in Peking," in *English Writings of Rabindranath Tagore,* Sisir K. Das, Ed. (New Delhi: Sahitya Akademi, 1996), rpt. 2008, Vol. II, p. 666.

What is striking is not just the vast oeuvre of his work, but its depth and quality. As Mohit Kumar Ray says in his Preface to his two-volume anthology of essays on Rabindranath, "Whatever he touched turned into gold."[3] As a multi-genre exponent, Rabindranath also wrote lectures, scholarly and discursive articles on diverse subjects and science tracts and primers. He founded and developed institutions and was thus an educationist, a rural reconstructionist, an environmentalist, one who established cooperatives and, in short, he was a nation builder and above all, a deep humanist and a man certainly for all times. Yet he was a traveller too, having taken on the task of being on a one-man mission of a cultural ambassador striving to bring the East and West closer creating universal understanding by promoting mutual respect. While he wrote in various genres, the one closest to his heart was the song, where words and melody combine in a perfect marriage of unmistakable harmony, giving them a universal resonance which is most apparent in his spiritual songs.

What Rabindranath wrote in his eighty years is a colossal body of work, which is not always possible for any one person to read in a lifetime, as well as analyze and interpret the entire body of his work. If he was not so close to us in time, people might have thought that his body of work could not have been written and accomplished by one man. They would have believed that he probably had a whole school of scribes and artists to write/create in his name. The fact that he found time to build institutions, write creative genres, lectures, scholarly and discursive articles on diverse subjects and edu-

3. Mohit K. Ray, *Studies on Rabindranath Tagore* (New Delhi: Atlantic Publishers and Distributors, 2004), Preface, Vol II, p. v.

cational texts (including primers—*Shahajpath*—the only Nobel Laureate to do so) and implement his vision through his multiple pragmatic projects, make him the true Renaissance man, the "myriad-minded" man as Coleridge says of Shakespeare, which is the title of Datta and Robinson's 1996 biography *Rabindranath Tagore*.

The advantage of growing up in the exciting creative atmosphere of the Tagore household shaped his love of the freedom of exercising his reason and imagination that found expression in the two institutions he established at Shantiniketan (Abode of Peace) and Sriniketan (Abode of Grace)—a nation builder's gift to the nation for education and rural resuscitation, respectively. In fact, when Tagore was asked what he had done that was unique about Shantiniketan, with his characteristic modesty he said that he was not conscious of having created anything special, but admitted that he had created a *paribesh*, an atmosphere, by which he meant an environment which encouraged a holistic growth and development of the mind which nurtures both reason and imagination in individuals, who can then build inclusive societies and nations. In "Ideals of Education" he speaks about an "atmosphere of aspiration [...] for the expansion of the human spirit"[4] and goes on to emphasize an "atmosphere of naturalness in our relationship with strangers, and the spirit of hospitality"[5] which welcomes the visitor/stranger in his university, Visva-Bharati, promoting

---

4. Rabindranath Tagore, "Ideals of Education" in *Sisir K. Das, Ed.*, Vol. III, p. 611.
5. Ibid., p. 612.

social inclusion and encouraging a healthy exchange of ideas, knowledge and expertise.

His life's cargo as held in his institution is what he refers to in a handwritten note given to Mahatma Gandhi on his last visit to Shantiniketan before the Poet's death. Tagore makes an urgent plea, "Accept this institution under your protection. Visva-Bharati [Tagore's international university] is like a vessel, which is carrying the cargo of my life's best treasure and I hope it may claim special care from my countrymen for its preservation." Gandhi, who was Tagore's close friend and compatriot, was, like Tagore, a votary of peace and non-violence. Gandhi concedes to Tagore's urgent request saying "Gurudev" (the divine teacher) was truly international because he was national, so his establishment was of national significance. The motto of Visva-Bharati, "*Yatra visvam bhavatieka nidam*"—where the whole world could meet in a single "nest"—signifies the spirit of welcome and exchange that the Poet proposed and practiced as a true internationalist with integrity in his multifaceted work.

At Jorasanko, the confluence of cultures was enriched and facilitated by readings in Sanskrit from the Upanishads, the poetry of Hafez in Persian, of English literary masters and the nurturing of and contribution to Bengali modern literature which flowered during the Bengal Renaissance. This cultural pluralism is what shaped and enriched Rabindranath's creativity. Rabindranath's deep immersion in and understanding of the Upanishads ensured his rootedness in Hindu philosophy. As an Indian, he was acutely aware of the multireligious reality of the country. At the age of twelve in 1873, he had accompanied his father, Maharashi Debendranath on one of his long journeys across India. During the trip, they stopped at Amritsar and joined in the hymns during services at the Golden Temple, where respect of the father for another religion's hymns and mode of worship (here Sikhism), was instilled in the young Rabindranath. We see Tagore's vast body of work being enriched by his knowledge and reverence for Buddhism in his dance dramas, *Chitrangada* (1882) and *Natir Puja* (1926), for Christ's life and passion in his poem, "The Child" (1930), for the Muslim position in Indian society in his novel, *Ghare Baire* (1916, *The Home and the World*) and the short story, "Mussalmanir Galpo" (1941, *The Story of a Muslim Woman*) and Zoroastrianism in his Hibbert Lectures delivered at Oxford and published in *The Religion of Man* (1931)—which are just a few examples of his multireligious interests and empathy.

It is this all-embracing approach to different religions and religious groups which constitute a confluence in the Poet, the meeting point of beliefs and faiths accounting for many of Rabindranath's poems and songs being addressed to a Supreme power, not identifiable with any specific religion, where the Poet appeals, addresses, questions or just converses with his creator using the intimate "Thou"/"Thy" in outpourings/confidences that are imbued with the anxiety, anguish, weariness or joy that life brings.

Many of these songs have been gathered later in a three volume collection, *Gitabitan* (1931, 1932, Revd. Edn. 1941, 1950) where they are classified under various titles, like "Puja" (Worship) and "Prem" (Love), the six seasons of Bengal, patriotic songs or dance dramas. However, critics, scholars and practitioners of Rabindranath's songs agree that many of the songs under Puja and Prem, could be put in either of the categories as they express a love that can be imagined for the Creator or a beloved. It is this ambiguity that makes these songs all the more poignant, where the love of God and of a person become interchangeable and even synonymous in a Poet, noted for his deep humanism.

When Rabindranath's mother, Sarala Devi died, the Poet was only thirteen; the sight of his father sitting still in meditation on the terrace near his room of seclusion, when his mother's body was being taken away for cremation, was a picture that would remain carved in the Poet's mind as an indelible memory in subsequent years, as he faced the death of many of this loved ones and confronted tragic events in his country and the world, leading him to seek meaning and strength in his inner life. Sabyasachi Bhattacharya has discussed the Poet's two levels of existence, his contemplative and meditative life which Rabindranath himself called his "Inner Life,"[6] distinguishable from the everyday, the Outer Life which is perceived and experienced through observation and an encounter requiring action. It is the acute and perceptive experience of the outer world, the environment, the social realities and events of local and global significance that leads the Poet to delve into his own inner recesses of interpretation and analysis where he finds solace in the calm and peace of his Inner Life, which often find expression in his songs.

Many of the poems in his Bengali collections, *Naibedya* (1901, "Offerings"), *Kheya* (1906, "The Ferry") and *Gitanjali* (1910) from which Rabindranath's English translations in the prose poems in *Gitanjali* (1912, "Song Offerings") are de-

---

6. Sabyasachi Bhattacharya, *Rabindranath Tagore: An Interpretation* (New Delhi: Penguin Viking, 2011), p. 7.

rived, are imbued with his deep, contemplative thoughts, addressed to a Supreme power in intimate confidences. William Radice comments on the "biblical" character of the English *Gitanjali*, not only in its phrasing, with the poems broken up into "verses" as in the Authorized Version of the English Bible (1611)[7] but also Rabindranath's Christ-like impression on those who saw and heard him at Rothenstein's home at Hampstead on July 7, 1912. However, the tides altered considerably in global responses to Rabindranath as he spoke out against rising militarization, colonial expansionism and ruthless capitalism globally, but many recognized and respected his spiritual and poetic integrity. In his work, Rabindranath promotes creative unity, facilitated by his imagination and capacity for service to others, born of human empathy and engendering a bond with all humanity. In *The Religion of Man* (1931), which carries his "message of universal humanism,"[8] the Poet postulates that man's humanity aligns him with the everlasting and his creative principle with the Creator. The nurturing of the creative principle is the guiding star of his school's vision, urging the creative spirit beyond "any custom-made religion" and differences of "caste or creed" in a system which promotes the "unity of truth."[9]

The selection of poems for the first edition of *The Heart of God* was made by Revd. Herbert F. Vetter who was the editor of the volume. In his insightful Introduction, Vetter mentions the collections of Tagore's work from which he chose the

---

7. Rabindranath Tagore, *Gitanjali*, Translated and edited by William Radice (New Delhi: Penguin Books, 2011), Introduction, p. xxxvii.

8. Bhattacharya, 2011, p. 184.

9. Quoted by Uma Dasgupta in *My Life in My Words*, p. 144.

poems. This expanded edition includes additional poems from *Gitanjali* (1912) and *The Gardener* (1913), from the collection of short and pithy verse in Tagore's *Fireflies* (1928) several from the collection *Poems* (1942), as well as the last section from Tagore's poem, "The Child" (1930), the only poem he wrote in English in a burst of creative energy inspired by the Passion of Christ play he witnessed at Oberammergau, Germany.

All the poems which have been added to this expanded edition are translations by the Poet himself. Revd. Vetter decided to give the poems descriptive titles, gleaned from each poem, rather than the numbers originally given by Rabindranath. The same method has been adopted for the additional poems included in this extended edition. Vetter also changed the "Thou" and "Thy" to "You" and "Your" with an eye to a modern readership, which has been followed by the publisher in the additional poems.

The final section from "The Child" is the penultimate poem in this book, as it looks forward to new birth, signifying renewal and redemption, offering solace and hope in these troubled times. In a chapter on the poem that I wrote earlier, I say that it is "the man from the East, who brings this message of peace in his recognition of The Child as the completion of the quest, can as the Seer confirms, 'I have seen!' The truth is revealed in this final affirmation of life's renewal...affirming Tagore's faith in man's intrinsic capacity for compassion that ensures life's continuity as one moves beyond conflict to peace."[10] This is what this selection seeks

10. Bashabi Fraser, "The Man of Faith: Tagore on Social Inclusion" in Blanka Knotkova-Capkova et. al., *Tagore on Discriminations* (Prague: Metropolitan

to convey—the Poet's message of peace and compassion. "A Hundred Years from Now" which is the closing poem here, reaffirms Rabindranath's relevance today, as we encounter his prescience and wisdom, reading him with full understanding and gratitude over a century later (it was published in 1913).

In Rabindranath, we witness a confluence of understanding and faith, stemming from his upbringing in the Thakurbari—the amalgamation of cultures and creativity in the Tagore household, where the Upanishads provided a guiding light to the members of this remarkable family who provided the impetus for the enlightenment that signified the Bengal/Indian Renaissance, the movement that propelled India into the modern era, of which Rabindranath Tagore was a leading light in its final chapter. Rabindranath concludes *The Religion of Man* with a section from the Upanishads, translated by himself, seeking someone who can embrace the needs of all people in all times, someone who "may ... unite us with the bond of truth, of common fellowship, of righteousness"[11]— in a confluence that is emblematic of the Poet's spiritual transnationalism. As a liberal humanist, Rabindranath, who was initially hailed as the Eastern Sage and Seer, was both a visionary and a pragmatist, guided by his innate spirituality. He identifies and was guided by his *Jiban Debata*, the "Lord of his Being" throughout his life, as he "lived by his faith in life, in humanity, in God."[12] We hope that together with all that is dependable and noble in human nature, Rabindranath Tagore's poems/songs, with their prayerful intensity and sincerity, will

University Prague Press, 2015), p. 54.
11. Sisir K. Das, Ed., Vol. III, 1996, p. 189.
12. Ibid., Vol II, p. 653.

survive the test of time with their universal appeal and ability to illuminate. To conclude, in the words of the Poet, his

> *... fancies are fireflies, —*
> *Specks of living light*
> *twinkling in the dark.*
> —*Fireflies*, No. 1

Dr. Bashabi Fraser, CBE
Professor Emerita of English and Creative Writing
Director, Scottish Centre of Tagore Studies
Edinburgh Napier University

Preface

Modern Indian thought makes a noble attempt to get really clear about itself in Rabindranath Tagore. Born in 1861, he is at the same time thinker, poet, and musician. He has himself translated his important works into English. The attention of Europe was directed to him by his becoming the recipient of the Nobel Prize for Literature in 1913. For many years he lived at Santiniketan, in Bengal, where he built up a school and college on modern educational lines.

With Tagore, ethical world and life affirmation has completely triumphed. It governs his worldview and will suffer nothing of world and life negation beside it. This has all the significance of a really great deed. A process of development that has been going on for centuries reaches in him its natural conclusion. He demands that we should belong to God with the soul and serve God actively in the world.

Joy in life and joy in creation belong, according to Tagore, to our human nature. He is as little able as the others who had attempted it before him to really found the worldview of ethical affirmation on knowledge of the universe. But the Goethe of India gives expression to his personal experience that this is the truth in a manner more profound and more powerful and more charming than anyone had ever done before. This completely noble and harmonious thinker belongs not only to his own people but to humanity.

—Albert Schweitzer

Introduction

All the black evils in the world have overflowed their banks,
   Yet, oarsmen, take your places with the blessing of
sorrow in your souls!
   Whom do you blame, brothers? Bow your heads down!
   The sin has been yours and ours.
   The heat growing in the heart of God for ages—
   The cowardice of the weak, the arrogance of the strong, the greed
of fat prosperity, the rancour of the wronged, pride of race, and insult
to man—
   Has burst God's peace, raging in storm.

I first found these lines during World War II—and have
never forgotten them. After the war, when I sought more of
Tagore's work, I first encountered his prayers of power. With
what other literature of my acquaintance might they be com-
pared? I saw kinship with the enduring majesty and inner
depths of the Hebrew Psalms, yet happily they avoided the
latter's recurring vindictiveness. I felt Tagore's passionate,
profoundly personal I-Thou experience akin to that expressed
in the Confessions of Augustine, yet he was no ally of St.
Augustine's intense negation of both life and the world. The
prayers of the modern Poet of India did and do celebrate life
in spite of its abundance of tragedy, and they affirm our world
of ever enduring, ever changing harmonies of color and sound.

When I met Amiya Chakravarty, an Indian and American
scholar who once was Tagore's literary secretary, he encour-

aged my quest to know more about this rare living legacy of prayer. I was clearly not alone in my appreciation of Tagore's contribution. Indeed, it was precisely such work as the prayers in this small book that led to Rabindranath's becoming the first Asian to be awarded the Nobel Prize for Literature in 1913. The Nobel Committee considered and passed over Tolstoy, Ibsen, Strindberg, Yeats, and George Bernard Shaw. The award symbolized the uncommon strength of Tagore's simple prayers of common life. Indeed, in his introduction to Rabindranath Tagore's first English writings, Gitanjali (Song Offerings), W. B. Yeats tells us that when he was carrying the manuscript with him as he traveled on trains and buses, he often had to close it lest some stranger see how much it moved him.

Tagore's poem prayers are moving affirmations of power that are not divorced from the tragedies of life. His mother died when he was thirteen. He lost his wife when she was only thirty. Soon thereafter, he experienced the death of a daughter as well as that of his father and his youngest son. Even before this devastating series of events came the disturbing death of his beloved sister-in-law, Kadambari, who took her own life. Rabindranath himself years later experienced a period of such depression and despair that he, too, considered ending his own life.

Nevertheless, like the fabled Phoenix bird arising from the ashes, Rabindranath emerged as a world-renowned person of power. Consider the astounding range of the work of this poet who was born in the mansion of a culturally distinguished Calcutta family on May 7, 1861. He was an educator who as a child so intensely hated going to school that he refused to continue to go, but he later established a liberating school for children at his family estate 100 miles from Calcutta in a place named by his father, the Abode of Peace. He later also founded there, in Santiniketan, an international university, Visva-Bharati, designed to foster an ongoing meeting of East and West to facilitate a creative synthesis of the arts and sciences, recreating civilization. As if that were not enough, in Tagore's lifelong labor to free his ailing country from domination by the British Empire, he helped establish lively centers of education for India's overwhelmingly illiterate population then living in poverty and disease-struck rural villages all across the land. The poet believed that India, the birthplace of such historic world religions as Hinduism and Buddhism, must meet the challenge of creative response to the Western civilization that was choking its development. He carried forward his father's and grandfather's leadership of the Hindu reform movement, known as the Brahmo Samaj, a major facilitator of the Indian Renaissance. He not only affirmed his Indian roots in the ancient Vedas, he affirmed that the Buddha was the greatest human being who ever lived; he extolled the Christian virtues of the Sermon on the Mount; and he translated the poems of Kabir, the daringly innovative mystic seer of Islam.

This exemplar of a new renaissance of Indian and world civilization lived an astonishingly adequate life. He was a poet and educator, a playwright and actor, a composer and singer, as well as a painter, essayist, novelist, and author of short stories. He was also both a social reformer who created a center for rural reconstruction and a world traveler who spoke to citizens of many nations in both the East and the West: China, Japan, Russia, the United States, France, Britain, Holland, Switzerland, Germany, Austria, Italy, Czechoslovakia, Norway,

Sweden, Denmark, Bulgaria, Persia, Egypt, and Greece. And he was an honored visitor to Southeast Asia, delighted to note the continuing impact of ancient India among these neighbors.

Shortly before Tagore's death in 1941 in Calcutta at the age of eighty, the chief justice of India presented this rebel ally of Mahatma Gandhi with an honorary doctorate awarded by Oxford University. The citation noted that the myriad-minded Dr. Tagore did not hold himself aloof from the dust and heat of the world; he did not fear to challenge the British Raj itself and the authority of the British Empire's magistrates. Tagore appreciatively accepted this recognition of his life work as "a happy augury of an Age to come."

I think humanity increasingly will honor the treasury of prayers breathed by this international exemplar of sacred power that is somewhere-nowhere-everywhere always. With this purpose in mind, I have prepared this deliberately small volume of durable literature presented in a form suitable for present-day use. Titles have been added to each selection. Whenever it was occasionally necessary to degenderize the text, I have done so in the spirit of Tagore. I have also edited the prayers in the language of contemporary daily speech, thereby avoiding such archaic obstacles as thee and thou.

The sources from which I have drawn these selections are *Gitanjali* (1912), *The Gardener* (1913), *Sadhana* (1913), *Fruit-Gathering* (1916), *Stray Birds* (1916), *Crossing* (1918), and *The Fugitive and Other Poems* (1921).

My own labor has been lightened by the excellent publication of *The English Writings of Rabindranath Tagore*, edited by Sisir Kumar Das: Volume 1, *Poems* (1994); Volume 2, *Plays, Stories, Essays* (1996).

For those who may be interested, there is a major admiring but sharply demythologizing biography published in 1995 entitled *Rabindranath Tagore: The Myriad-Minded Man*, by Krishna Dutta and Andrew Robinson.

I wish to thank my esteemed colleagues in ministry who advised me on the Tagore prayers as part of a larger project: Dr. Arthur Foote of S.W. Harbor, Maine; Professor John F. Hayward of Southern Illinois University; the Reverend Kenneth Read-Brown of the First Parish (Old Ship Church) in Hingham, Massachusetts; and the Reverend Bruce Southworth of the Community Church of New York. Esteemed advisors in the field of publishing include Jeanette Hopkins, Gobin and Julia Stair, Marie Cantlon, and the staff of Michael Kerber, at Tuttle Publishing.

Finally, the spirit of *The Heart of God* may be symbolized by a single sentence by Sarvepalli Radhakrishnan, the distinguished philosopher and statesman who served as president of India:

Rabindranath Tagore was one of the few representatives of the universal person to whom the future of the world belongs.

—H.F.V.
Cambridge, Massachusetts
April 23, 1997

Prayers

Companion of the Companionless

Here is your footstool and there rest your feet where live the poorest, and lowliest, and lost.

When I try to bow to you, my obeisance cannot reach down to the depth where your feet rest among the poorest, and lowliest, and lost.

Pride can never approach to where you walk in the clothes of the humble among the poorest, and lowliest, and lost.

My heart can never find its way to where you keep company with the companionless among the poorest, the lowliest, and the lost.

Accept Me

Accept me, dear God, accept me for this while.

Let those orphaned days that passed without You be forgotten.

Only spread this little moment wide across Your lap, holding it under Your light.

I have wandered in pursuit of voices that drew me, yet led me nowhere.

Now let me sit in peace and listen to Your words in the soul of my silence.

Do not turn away Your face from my heart's dark secrets, but burn them till they are alight with Your fire.

A Question to God

Age after age, O God, You have sent Your messengers into this pitiless world, who have left their word: "Forgive all. Love all. Cleanse your hearts from the blood-red stains of hatred."

Adorable are they, ever to be remembered; yet from the outer door, I have turned them away today—this evil day—with unmeaning salutation.

Have I not seen secret malignance strike down the helpless under the cover of hypocritical might?

Have I not heard the silenced voice of justice weeping in solitude at might's defiant outrages?

Have I not seen in what agony reckless youth, running mad, has vainly shattered its life against insensitive rocks?

Choked is my voice, mute are my songs today, and darkly my world lies imprisoned in a dismal dream; and I ask You, O God, in tears, "Have You Yourself forgiven, have even You loved those who are poisoning Your air and blotting out Your light?"

In Your Eyes

My heart, the bird of the wilderness, has found its sky in your eyes.

They are the cradle of the morning, they are the kingdom of the stars.

My songs are lost in their depths.

Let me but soar in that sky, in its lonely immensity.

Let me but cleave its clouds and spread wings in its sunshine.

Why?

At midnight the would-be ascetic announced: "This is the time to give up my home and seek God. Ah, who has held me so long in delusion here?"

God whispered, "I," but the ears of the man were stopped.

With a baby asleep at her breast lay his wife, peacefully sleeping on one side of the bed.

The man said, "Who are you that have fooled me so long?"

The voice again said, "They are God," but he heard it not.

The baby cried out in its dream, nestling close to its mother.

God commanded, "Stop, don't leave your home," but still he heard not.

God sighed and complained, "Why does my servant wander to seek me, forsaking me?"

Notes from the Other Shore

I must launch out my boat. The languid hours pass by on the shore—Alas for me!

The spring has done its flowering and taken leave. And now with the burden of faded futile flowers I wait and linger.

The waves have become clamorous, and upon the bank in the shady lane the yellow leaves flutter and fall.

What emptiness do you gaze upon! Do you not feel a thrill passing through the air with the notes of the far-away song floating from the other shore?

Trees

Be still, my heart, these great trees are prayers.

My Greetings

Comrade of the road, here are my traveler's greetings to You.

God of my broken heart, of leave-taking and loss, of the gray silence of the dayfall, my greetings of the ruined house to You.

Light of the newborn morning, sun of the everlasting day, my greetings of undying hope to You.

My Guide, I am a wayfarer on an endless road, my greetings of a wanderer to You.

Face to Face?

Day after day, O Ruler of my life, shall I stand before You face to face?

With folded hands, O Ruler of all worlds, shall I stand before You face to face?

Under Your great sky, in solitude and silence with humble heart, shall I stand before You face to face?

In this laborious world of Yours, tumultuous with toil and with struggle, among hurrying crowds, shall I stand before You face to face?

And when my work shall be done in this world, O Ruler of rulers, alone and speechless, shall I stand before You face to face?

The Last Song

Then finish the last song and let us leave.
Forget this night when the night is no more.
Whom do I try to clasp in my arms?
Dreams can never be made captive.

My eager hands press emptiness to my heart
and it bruises my breast.

Death

Death, Your servant, is at my door. He has crossed the unknown sea and brought Your call to my home.

The night is dark, and my heart is fearful—yet I shall take up the lamp, open my gates, and bow to him my welcome. It is Your messenger who stands at my door.

I shall worship him with folded hands and with tears. I shall worship him, placing at his feet the treasure of my heart.

Hold My Hand

Deliver me from my own shadows, O God, from the wreck and confusion of my days, for the night is dark and Your pilgrim is blinded.

Hold my hand.

Deliver me from despair.
Touch with Your flame the lightless lamp of my sorrow.
Waken my tired strength from its sleep.
Do not let me linger behind, counting my losses.
Let the road sing to me of the house at every step.
For the night is dark, and Your pilgrim is blinded.

Hold my hand.

Deliverance

Deliverance is not for me in renunciation.
I feel the embrace of freedom in a thousand bonds
of delight.

You ever pour for me the fresh draft of Your
wine of various colors and fragrances, filling this
earthen vessel to the brim.

My world will light its hundred different
lamps with Your flame and place them before the
altar of Your temple.

No, I will never shut the doors of my senses.
The delights of sight and hearing and touch will
bear Your delight.

Yes, all my illusions will burn into
illumination of joy, and all my desires ripen into
fruits of love.

This Is My Prayer

Give me the supreme courage of love, this is my prayer—the courage to speak, to do, to suffer at Your will, to leave all things or be left alone. Strengthen me on errands of danger, honor me with pain, and help me climb to that difficult mood that sacrifices daily to You.

Give me the supreme confidence of love, this is my prayer—the confidence that belongs to life in death, to victory in defeat, to the power hidden in the frailest beauty, to that dignity in pain which accepts hurt but disdains to return it.

The Rebel

I came nearest to You, though I did not know it, when I came to hurt You.

I owned You at last as my Master when I fought against You to be defeated.

I merely made my debt to You burdensome when I robbed You in secret.

I struggled in my pride against Your current, only to feel all Your force in my breast.

Rebelliously, I put out the light in my house, and Your sky surprised me with its stars.

By All Means

By all means they try to hold me secure who love me in this world.

But it is otherwise with your love which is greater than theirs,

and you keep me free.

Lest I forget them they never venture to leave me alone.

But day passes by after day and you are not seen.

If I call not you in my prayers, if I keep not you in my heart,

your love for me still waits for my love.

Time to Sit Quietly

I ask for a moment's indulgence to sit by Your side. The works that I have in hand I will finish afterward.

Away from the sight of Your face, my heart knows no rest or respite, and my work becomes an endless toil in a shoreless sea of toil.

Today the summer has come at my window with its sighs and murmurs; and the bees are plying their minstrelsy at the court of the flowering grove.

Now it is time to sit quietly, face to face with You, and to sing dedication of life in this silent and overflowing leisure.

Are You Abroad on this Stormy Night?

Are you abroad on this stormy night on your journey of love, my friend?

The sky groans like one in despair.

I have no sleep tonight.

Ever and again I open my door and look out on the darkness, my friend!

I can see nothing before me.

I wonder where lies your path!

By what dim shore of the ink-black river, by what far edge of the frowning forest, through what mazy depth of gloom art you threading your course to come to me, my friend?

Traveler, Must You Go?

Traveler, must you go?

The night is still and the darkness swoons upon the forest.

The lamps are bright in our balcony, the flowers all fresh, and the youthful eyes still awake.

Is the time for your parting come?

Traveler, must you go?

We have not bound your feet with our entreating arms.

Your doors are open. Your horse stands saddled at the gate.

If we have tried to bar your passage it was but with our songs.

Did we ever try to hold you back it was but with our eyes.

Traveler, we are helpless to keep you. We have only our tears.

What quenchless fire glows in your eyes?
What restless fever runs in your blood?
What call from the dark urges you?

What awful incantation have you read among the stars in the sky, that with a sealed secret message the night entered your heart, silent and strange?

If you do not care for merry meetings, if you must have peace, weary heart, we shall put our lamps out and silence our harps.

We shall sit still in the dark in the rustle of leaves, and the tired moon will shed pale rays on your window.

O traveler, what sleepless spirit has touched you from the heart of the midnight?

The Least Grain of Corn

I had gone a-begging from door to door in the village path, when Your golden chariot appeared in the distance like a gorgeous dream, and I wondered who was this King of all kings!

My hopes rose high, and I thought my evil days were at an end. I stood waiting for alms to be given unasked and for wealth to be scattered on all sides in the dust.

The chariot stopped where I stood. Your glance fell on me, and You came down with a smile. I felt that the luck of my life had come at last. Then all of a sudden You held out Your right hand, saying, "What have you to give me?"

Ah, what a kingly jest was it to open Your palm to a beggar to beg! I was confused and stood undecided, and then from my wallet I slowly took out the least little grain of corn and gave it to You.

How great was my surprise when at the day's end, I emptied my bag on the floor only to find a least little grain of gold among the poor heap! I bitterly wept and wished that I had the heart to give You my all.

My Friend

I have come to You to take Your touch before I begin my day.

Let Your eyes rest upon my eyes for a while.

Let me take to my work the assurance of Your comradeship, my Friend.

Fill my mind with Your music to last through the desert of noise.

Let Your love's sunshine kiss the peaks of my thoughts and linger in my life's valley where the harvest ripens.

My Polar Star

I have made You the polar star of my existence; never again can I lose my way in the voyage of life.

Wherever I go, You are always there to shower Your beneficence all around me. Your face is ever present before my mind's eyes.

If I lose sight of You even for a moment, I almost lose my mind.

Whenever my heart is about to go astray, just a glance of You makes it feel ashamed of itself.

Not Altogether Lost

I know that this life, missing its ripeness in love, is not altogether lost.

I know that the flowers that fade in the dawn, the streams that strayed in the desert, are not altogether lost.

I know that whatever lags behind, in this life laden with slowness, is not altogether lost.

I know that my dreams that are still unfulfilled, and my melodies still unstruck, are clinging to Your lute strings, and they are not altogether lost.

Wisdom

I have scaled the peak and found no shelter in fame's bleak and barren height.

Lead me, my Guide, before the light fades, into the valley of quiet where life's harvest mellows into golden wisdom.

Where Do You Hurry?

Where do you hurry with your basket this late evening when the marketing is over?

They all have come home with their burdens; the moon peeps from above the village trees.

The echoes of the voices calling for the ferry run across the dark water to the distant swamp where wild ducks sleep.

Where do you hurry with your basket when the marketing is over?

Sleep has laid her fingers upon the eyes of the earth.

The nests of the crows have become silent, and the murmurs of the bamboo leaves are silent.

The laborers home from their fields spread their mats in the courtyards.

Where do you hurry with your basket when the marketing is over?

Your Presence

I know not from what distant time You are ever coming nearer to meet me.

Your sun and Your stars can never keep You hidden from me forever.

In many a morning and evening, Your footsteps have been heard, and Your messenger has come within my heart and called me in secret.

I know not why today my life is all astir, and a feeling of tremulous joy is passing through my heart.

It is as if my time were come to wind up my work, and I feel in the air a faint sweet smell of Your presence.

Treasures

I know that the day will come when my sight of this earth shall be lost, and life will take its leave in silence, drawing the last curtain over my eyes.

Yet stars will watch at night, and morning rise as before, and hours heave like sea waves casting up pleasures and pains.

When I think of this end of my moments, the barrier of the moments breaks, and I see by the light of death Your world with its careless treasures. Rare is its lowliest seat; rare is its meanest of lives.

Things that I longed for in vain and things that I got—let them pass. Let me but truly possess the things that I ever spurned and overlooked.

Dweller in My Endless Dreams

You are the evening cloud floating in the sky of my dreams.

I paint you and fashion you ever with my love longings.

You are my own, my own, Dweller in my endless dreams!

Your feet are rosy-red with the glow of my heart's desire, Gleaner of my sunset songs!

Your lips are bitter-sweet with the taste of my wine of pain.

You are my own, my own, Dweller in my lonesome dreams!

With the shadow of my passion have I darkened your eyes, Haunter of the depth of my gaze!

I have caught you and wrapt you, my love, in the net of my music.

You are my own, my own, Dweller in my deathless dreams!

My Voyage

I thought that my voyage had come to its end at the last limit of my power, that the path before me was closed, that provisions were exhausted and the time had come to take shelter in a silent obscurity.

But I find that Your will knows no end in me, and when old words die out on the tongue, new melodies break forth from the heart; and where the old tracks are lost, new country is revealed with its wonders.

Our Master

Our master is a worker and we work with him.

Boisterous is his mirth and we laugh with his laughter.

He beats his drum and we march.

He sings and we dance in its tune.

His play is of life and death.

We stake our joys and sorrows and play with him.

His call comes like the rumbling of clouds; we set out to cross oceans and hills.

Your Name

I will utter Your name, sitting alone among the shadows of my silent thoughts. I will utter it without words; I will utter it without purpose. For I am like a child that calls its mother a hundred times, glad that it can say, "Mother."

You Are There

I would leave this chanting and singing and telling of beads. Whom do I worship in this lonely dark corner of a temple with doors all shut? I open my eyes and see that, You, O God, are not before me.

You are there where the tiller is tilling the hard ground and where the pathmaker is breaking stones. You are with them in sun and in shower, and Your garment is covered with dust. I put off my holy mantle and even, like You, come down on the dusty soil.

Deliverance? Where is deliverance to be found? You Yourself have joyfully taken upon Yourself the bonds of creation; You are bound with us all forever.

I come out of my meditations and leave aside my flowers and incense. What harm if my clothes become tattered and stained? I meet You and stand by You in toil and in the sweat of my brow.

My Heart Is on Fire

My heart is on fire with the flame of your songs.
It spreads and knows no bounds.

It dances swinging its arms in the sky, burning up the dead and the decaying.

The silent stars watch it from across the darkness.

The drunken winds come rushing upon it from all sides.

O, this fire, like a red lotus, spreads its petals in the heart of the night.

Beyond Despair

In desperate hope, I go and search for her in all the corners of my room; I find her not.

My house is small, and what once has gone from it can never be regained.

But infinite is Your mansion, my God; and seeking her, I have come to Your door.

I stand under the golden canopy of Your evening sky, and I lift my eager eyes to Your face.

I have come to the brink of eternity from which nothing can vanish—no hope, no happiness, no vision of a face seen through tears.

Oh, dip my emptied life into that ocean, plunge it into the deepest fullness. Let me, for once, feel that lost, sweet touch in the allness of the universe.

Forgive My Languor, O Lord

Forgive my languor, O Lord,
if ever I lag behind
    upon life's way.

Forgive my anguished heart
which trembles and hesitates
    in its service.

Forgive my fondness
that lavishes its wealth
    upon an unprofitable past.

Forgive these faded flowers
    in my offering
that wilt in the fierce heat
    of panting hours.

My Song

In my songs, I have voiced Your spring flowers and given rhythm to Your rustling leaves.

I have sung into the hush of Your night and the peace of Your morning.

The thrill of the first summer rains has passed into my tunes and the waving of the autumn harvest.

Let not my song cease.

Salutation

In one salutation to You, my God, let all my senses spread out and touch this world at Your feet.

Like a raincloud hung low with its burden of unshed showers, let all my mind bend down at Your door in one salutation to You.

Let all my songs gather together their diverse strains into a single current and flow to a sea of silence in one salutation to You.

Like a flock of homesick cranes flying night and day back to their mountain nests, let all my life take its voyage to its eternal home in one salutation to You.

The Solitary Wayfarer

In the deep shadows of the rain, with secret steps, You walk, silent as night, eluding all watchers.

Today the morning has closed its eyes, heedless of the insistent calls of the loud east wind, and a thick veil has been drawn over the ever wakeful blue sky.

The woodlands have hushed their songs, and doors are shut at every house. You are the solitary wayfarer in this deserted street. Oh, my only Friend, my best Beloved, the gates are open in my house. Do not pass by like a dream.

Sleep

In the night of weariness, let me give myself up to sleep without struggle, resting my trust upon You.

Let me not force my flagging spirit into a poor preparation for Your worship.

It is You who draws the veil of night upon the tired eyes of the day to renew its sight in a fresher gladness of awakening.

My Journey Is Long

The time that my journey takes is long and the way of it long.

I came out on the chariot of the first gleam of light, and pursued my voyage through the wildernesses of worlds leaving my track on many a star and planet.

It is the most distant course that comes nearest to yourself, and that training is the most intricate which leads to the utter simplicity of a tune.

The traveler has to knock at every alien door to come to his own, and one has to wander through all the outer worlds to reach the innermost shrine at the end.

My eyes strayed far and wide before I shut them and said "Here you are!"

The question and the cry "Oh, where?" melt into tears of a thousand streams and deluge the world with the flood of the assurance "I am!"

Mother Earth

Infinite wealth is not Yours, my patient and dusky mother dust!

You toil to fill the mouths of Your children, but food is scarce.

The gift of gladness that You have for us is never perfect.

You cannot satisfy all our hunger hopes, but should I desert You for that?

Your smile, which is shadowed with pain, is sweet to my eyes.

Your love, which knows not fulfillment, is dear to my heart.

From Your breast You have fed us with life but not immortality, which is why Your eyes are ever wakeful.

For ages You are working with color and song, yet Your heaven is not built, but only its sad suggestion.

Over Your creations of beauty, there is the mist of tears.

I will pour my songs into Your tender face and love Your mournful dust, Mother Earth.

Abounding Joy

Is it beyond You to be glad with the gladness of this rhythm? To be tossed and lost and broken in the whirl of this fearful joy?

All things rush on, they stop not, they look not behind; no power can hold them back, they rush on.

Keeping steps with that restless, rapid music, seasons come dancing and pass away—colors, tunes, and perfumes pour in endless cascades in the abounding joy that scatters and gives up and dies every moment.

Worker of the Universe

It is only the revelation of You as the Infinite that is endlessly new and eternally beautiful in us and that gives the only meaning to our self when we feel Your rhythmic throb as soul-life, the whole world in our own souls; then are we free.

O Worker of the universe! Let the irresistible current of Your universal energy come like the impetuous south wind of spring; let it come rushing over the vast field of human life. Let our newly awakened powers cry out for unlimited fulfillment in leaf and flower and fruit.

The Song that I Came to Sing

The song that I came to sing remains unsung to this day.

I have spent my days in stringing and in unstringing my instrument.

The time has not come true, the words have not been rightly set; only there is the agony of wishing in my heart.

The blossom has not opened; only the wind is sighing by.

I have not seen his face, nor have I listened to his voice; only I have heard his gentle footsteps from the road before my house.

The livelong day has passed in spreading his seat on the floor; but the lamp has not been lit and I cannot ask him into my house.

I live in the hope of meeting with him; but this meeting is not yet.

My Last Song

Let all the strains of joy mingle in my last song—the joy that makes the earth flow over in the riotous excess of the grass; the joy that sets the twin brothers, life and death, dancing over the wide world; the joy that sweeps in with the tempest, shaking and waking all life with laughter; the joy that sits still with its tears on the open, red lotus of pain; and the joy that throws everything it has upon the dust and knows not a word.

The Grasp of Your Hand

Let me not pray to be sheltered from dangers, but to be fearless in facing them.

Let me not beg for the stilling of my pain, but for the heart to conquer it.

Let me not crave in anxious fear to be saved, but hope for the patience to win my freedom.

Grant me that I may not be a coward, feeling Your mercy in my success alone; but let me find the grasp of Your hand in my failure.

Let My Song Be Simple

Let my song be simple as the waking in the morning, as the dripping of dew from the leaves,

Simple as the colors in clouds and showers of rain in the midnight.

But my lute strings are newly strung, and they darken their notes like spears sharp in their newness.

Thus they miss the spirit of the wind and hurt the light of the sky, and these strains of my songs fight hard to push back Your own music.

My All

Let only that little be left of me whereby I may name You my all.

Let only that little be left of my will whereby I may feel You on every side and come to You in everything and offer to You my love every moment.

Let only that little be left of me whereby I may never hide You.

Let only that little of my fetters be left whereby I am bound with Your will, and Your purpose is carried out in my life—and that is the fetter of Your love.

My Country

Let the earth and the water, the air and the fruits of my country be sweet, my God.

Let the homes and marts, the forests and fields of my country be full, my God.

Let the promises and hopes, the deeds and words of my country be true, my God.

Let the lives and hearts of the sons and daughters of my country be one, my God.

My Last Word

Let this be my last word, that I trust in Your love.

The Secret of Your Heart

Do not keep to yourself the secret of your heart, my friend!

Say it to me, only to me, in secret.

You who smile so gently, softly whisper, my heart will hear it, not my ears.

The night is deep, the house is silent, the birds' nests are shrouded with sleep.

Speak to me through hesitating tears, through faltering smiles, through sweet shame and pain, the secret of your heart!

Your Love

Let Your love play upon my voice and rest on my silence.

Let it pass through my heart into all my movements.

Let Your love, like stars, shine in the darkness of my sleep and dawn in my awakening.

Let it burn in the flame of my desires and flow in all currents of my own love.

Let me carry Your love in my life as a harp does its music, and give it back to You at last with my life.

Life of My Life

Life of my life, I shall ever try to keep my body pure, knowing that Your living touch is upon all my limbs.

I shall ever try to keep all untruths from my thoughts, knowing that You are that truth which has kindled the light of reason in my mind.

I shall ever try to drive all evils away from my heart and keep my love in flower, knowing that You have Your seat in the inmost shrine of my heart.

It shall be my endeavor to reveal You in my actions, knowing it is Your power that gives me strength to act.

Light

Light, my light, the world-filling light, the eye-kissing light, the heart-sweetening light:

Ah, the light dances, my Darling, at the center of my life; the light strikes, my Darling, the chords of my love; the sky opens; the wind runs wild; laughter passes over the earth.

The butterflies spread their sails on the sea of light. Lilies and jasmine surge up on the crest of the waves of light.

The light is shattered into gold on every cloud, my Darling, and it scatters gems in profusion.

Mirth spreads from leaf to leaf, my Darling, and gladness without measure. The heaven's river has drowned its banks, and the flood of joy is abroad.

If You Could Have It So

If you would have it so, I will end my singing.

If it sets your heart aflutter, I will take away my eyes from your face.

If it suddenly startles you in your walk, I will step aside and take another path.

If it confuses you in your flower-weaving, I will shun your lonely garden.

If it makes the water wanton and wild, I will not row my boat by your bank.

The Fullness of Peace

Not for me is the love that knows no restraint and is like foaming wine that, having burst its vessel in a moment, would run to waste.

Send me the love that is cool and pure like Your rain, which blesses the thirsty earth and fills the homely earthen jars.

Send me the love that would soak down into the center of being, and from there would spread like the unseen sap through the branching tree of life, giving birth to fruits and flowers.

Send me the love that keeps the heart still with the fullness of peace.

Obstinate Are the Shackles

Obstinate are the shackles, and my heart aches when I try to break them.

Freedom is all I want; but to hope for it, I feel ashamed.

I am certain that priceless wealth is in You and that You are my best friend, but I have not the heart to sweep away the tinsel that fills my room.

The shroud that covers me is a shroud of dust and death; I hate it, yet hug it in love.

My debts are large, my failures great, my shame secret and heavy; yet when I come to ask for my good, I quake in fear lest my prayer be granted.

Lost Time

On many an idle day I have grieved over lost time, but it is never lost, O God. You have taken every moment of my life in Your own hands.

Hidden in the heart of things, You are nourishing seeds into sprouts, buds into blossoms, and ripening flowers into fruitfulness.

I was tired and sleeping on my idle bed and imagined all work had ceased. In the morning, I awoke and found my garden full with wonders of flowers.

The Infinity of Your Love

Stand before my eyes, and let Your glance touch my songs into a flame.

Stand among Your stars, and let me find kindled in their lights my own fire of worship.

The earth is waiting at the world's wayside.

Stand upon the green mantle she has flung upon Your path, and let me find in her grass and meadow flowers the spread of my own salutation.

Stand in my lonely evening when my heart watches alone; fill her cup of solitude, and let me feel in myself the infinity of Your love.

God and the Devil

God seeks comrades and claims love,
the Devil seeks slaves and claims obedience.

I Want You, Only You

That I want You, only You—let my heart repeat without end. All desires that distract me, day and night, are false and empty to the core.

As the night keeps hidden in its gloom the petition for light, even thus in the depth of my unconsciousness rings the cry "I want You, only You."

As the storm still seeks its end in peace when it strikes against peace with all its might, even thus my rebellion strikes against Your love and still its cry is "I want You, only You."

The Immortal

Jewel-like the immortal
does not boast of its length of years
but of the scintillating point of its moment.

Rain

The day is dim with rain.

Angry lightning glances through the tattered cloud-veils, and the forest is like a caged lion shaking its mane in despair.

On such a day amid the winds beating their wings, let me find my peace in Your presence.

For the sorrowing sky has shadowed my solitude, to deepen the meaning of Your touch about my heart.

Darkness and Light

The lantern that I carry in my hand makes an enemy of the darkness of the farther road.

And this wayside becomes a terror to me, where even the flowering tree frowns like a spectre of scowling menace; and the sound of my own steps comes back to me in the echo of muffled suspicion.

Therefore, I pray for Your own morning light, when the far and the near will kiss each other, and life will be one in love.

The Stream of Life

The same stream of life that runs through my veins night and day runs through the world and dances in rhythmic measures.

It is the same life that shoots in joy through the dust of the earth in numberless blades of grass and breaks into tumultuous waves of leaves and flowers.

It is the same life that is rocked in the ocean-cradle of birth and of death, in ebb and in flow.

I feel my limbs made glorious by the touch of this world of life. And my pride is from the life-throb of ages dancing in my blood this moment.

Strike at the Root

This is my prayer to You, O God—strike, strike at the root of poverty in my heart.

Give me the strength to bear lightly my joys and sorrows.

Give me the strength to make my love fruitful in service.

Give me the strength never to disown the poor or bend my knees before insolent might.

Give me the strength to raise my mind high above daily trifles.

Give me the strength to surrender my strength to Your will with love.

The Lake

The lake lies low by the hill,
a tearful entreaty of love
at the foot of the inflexible.

Thanksgiving

Those who walk on the path of pride, crushing the lowly life under their tread, covering the tender green of the earth with their footprints in blood,

Let them rejoice and thank You, God, for the day is theirs.

But I am thankful that my lot lies with the humble who suffer and bear the burden of power and hide their faces and stifle their sobs in the dark.

For every throb of their pain has pulsed in the secret depth of Your night, and every insult has been gathered into Your great silence;

And the morrow is theirs.

. . .

O Sun, arise upon the bleeding hearts blossoming in flowers of the morning, and the torchlight revelry of pride shrunken to ashes.

Take, O Take

Time after time I came to Your gate with raised hands, asking for more and yet more.

You gave and gave, now in slow measure, now in sudden excess.

I took some, and some things I let drop; some lay heavy on my hands; some I made into playthings and broke them when I tired, till the wrecks and the hoard of Your gifts grew immense, hiding You, and the ceaseless expectation wore my heart out.

"Take, O take" has now become my cry.

Hold my hands; raise me from the still-gathering heap of Your gifts into the bare infinity of Your uncrowded presence.

Time

Time is endless in Your hands, O God. There is none to count Your minutes.

Days and nights pass, and ages bloom and fade like flowers. You know how to wait.

Your centuries follow one another in perfecting a small wildflower.

We have no time to lose, and having no time, we must scramble for our chances. We are too poor to be late.

Thus it is that time goes by, while I give it to every querulous person who claims it, and Your altar is empty of all offerings to the last.

At the end of the day, I hasten in fear lest the gate be shut, but I find that there is yet time.

The Trees and Grass

I have thanked the trees that have made my
life fruitful
But have failed to remember the grass
That has ever kept it green

Tears of the Earth

We rejoice, O God, that the tears of the earth keep her smiles in bloom.

The Stars

The stars crowd round the virgin night
in silent awe at her loneliness
that can never be touched.

What Divine Drink

What divine drink would You have, my God, from this overflowing cup of my life?

My Poet, is it Your delight to see Your creation through my eyes, to stand at the portals of my ears, to listen silently to Your own eternal harmony?

Your world is weaving words in my mind, and Your joy is adding music to them. You give Yourself to me in love and then feel Your own entire sweetness in me.

The Music of Love

When all the strings of my life will be tuned, then at every touch of Yours will come out the music of love.

No Night of Ease

When I awake in Your love, my night of ease will be ended.

Your sunrise will touch my heart with its touchstone of fire, and my voyage will begin in its orbit of triumphant suffering.

I shall dare to take up death's challenge and carry Your voice into the heart of mockery and menace.

I shall bare my breast against the wrongs hurled at Your children and take the risk of standing by Your side, where none but You remains.

O World

When my heart did not kiss You in love,
O World, Your light missed its full splendor and
Your sky watched through the long night with its
lighted lamp.

My heart came with her songs to Your side,
whispers were exchanged, and she put her wreath
on Your neck.

I know she has given You something which
will be treasured with Your stars.

The Cloud

The cloud gives all its gold
to the departing sun
and greets the rising moon
with only a pale smile.

Playtime

When my play was with You, I never questioned who You were. I knew no shyness or fear; my life was boisterous.

In the early morning, You would call me from my sleep like my own comrade and lead me running from glade to glade.

On those days, I never cared to know the meaning of songs You sang to me. Only my voice took up the tunes, and my heart danced in their cadences.

Now, when the playtime is over, what is this sudden sight that is come upon me? The world, with eyes bent upon Your feet, stands in awe with all its silent stars.

When the Heart Is Hard

When the heart is hard and parched, come upon me with a shower of mercy.

When grace is lost from life, come with a burst of song.

When tumultuous work raises its din on all sides, shutting me out from beyond, come to me, God of silence, with Your peace and rest.

When my beggarly heart sits crouched, shut up in a corner, break open the door, my God.

When desire blinds the mind with delusion and dust, O Holy One, come with Your light and Your thunder.

Ocean of Things

Thou ocean of things, they say, in your dark depths there are pearls and gems without end.

Many a diver learned in the sea is seeking for them.

But I care not to join in their search.

The light that flashes on your surface, the mystery that heaves on your bosom, the music that maddens your waves, and the dance that trips on your foam, are enough for me.

If ever I am weary of them, I will plunge into your unfathomed bottom where there is death, or the treasure.

Singing

When You command me to sing, it seems that my heart would break with pride; and I look to Your face, and tears come to my eyes.

All that is harsh and dissonant in my life melts into one sweet harmony—and my adoration spreads wings like a glad bird on its flight across the sea.

I know You take pleasure in my singing. I know that only as a singer I come before Your presence.

I touch, by the edge of the far-spreading wing of my song, Your feet, which I could never aspire to reach.

Drunk with the joy of singing, I forget myself, and call You Friend who is my Ruler.

When You Save Me

When You save me, the steps are lighter in the march of Your worlds.

When stains are washed away from my heart, it brightens the light of Your sun.

That the bud has not blossomed in beauty in my life spreads sadness in the heart of creation.

When the shroud of darkness will be lifted from my soul, it will bring music to Your smile.

Let My Country Awake

Where the mind is without fear, and the head is held high;

Where knowledge is free;

Where the world has not been broken up into fragments by narrow domestic walls;

Where words come out from the depth of truth;

Where tireless striving stretches its arms toward perfection;

Where the clear stream of reason has not lost its way into the dreary desert sand of dead habit;

Where the mind is led forward by You into ever widening thought and action—

Into that haven of freedom, my Father, let my country awake.

In the Silence of My Heart

You shall dwell in silence in my heart like the full moon in the summer night.

Your sad eyes shall watch over me in my wanderings.

The shadow of your veil shall rest upon my heart.

Your breath like the full moon in the summer night shall hover about my dreams, making them fragrant.

Nothing But Your Love

Yes, I know, this is nothing but Your love, O Beloved of my heart—this golden light that dances upon the leaves, these idle clouds sailing across the sky, this passing breeze leaving its coolness upon my forehead.

The morning light has flooded my eyes—this is Your message to my heart. Your face is bent from above, Your eyes look down on my eyes, and my heart has touched Your feet.

The Sky and the Nest

You are the sky, and You are the nest as well.

Beautiful One, there in the nest Your love encloses the soul with colors and sounds and odors.

There comes the morning, with the golden basket in her right hand bearing the wreath of beauty, silently to crown the earth.

And there comes the evening over the lonely meadows deserted by herds, through trackless paths, carrying cool drafts of peace in her golden pitcher from the western ocean of rest.

But there, where spreads the infinite sky for the soul to take her flight in, reigns the stainless white radiance. There is no day or night, no form or color, and never, never a word.

Now in the Evening

You have given me a seat at Your window from the early hour.

I have spoken to Your silent servants of the road running on Your errands and have sung with Your choir of the sky.

I have seen the sea in calm, bearing its immeasurable silence, and in storm, struggling to break open its own mystery of depth.

I have watched the earth in its prodigal feast of youth and in its slow hours of brooding shadows.

Those who went to sow seeds have heard my greetings, and those who brought their harvest home, or their empty baskets, have passed by my songs.

Thus at last my day has ended, and now in the evening, I sing my last song to say that I have loved Your world.

I Threw Away My Heart

I threw away my heart in the world; you took it up.

I sought for joy and gathered sorrow, you gave me sorrow and I found joy.

My heart was scattered in pieces, you picked them up in your hand and strung them in a thread of love.

You let me wander from door to door to show me at last how near you are.

Your love plunged me into the deep trouble.

When I raised my head I found I was at your door.

Gifts

You have given me Your love, filling the world with Your gifts.

They are showered upon me when I do not know them, for my heart is asleep, and dark is the night.

Though lost in the cavern of my dreams, I have been thrilled with gladness;

And I know that in return for the treasure of Your great worlds, You will receive from me one little flower of love in the morning when my heart awakes.

You Have Made Me Endless

You have made me endless, such is Your pleasure. This frail vessel You empty again and again, and fill it ever with fresh life.

This little flute of a reed You have carried over hills and dales and have breathed through it melodies eternally new.

At the immortal touch of Your hands, my little heart loses its limits in joy and gives birth to utterance ineffable.

Your infinite gifts come to me only on these very small hands of mine. Ages pass, and still You pour, and still there is room to fill.

Friends Whom I Knew Not

You have made me known to friends whom I knew not. You have given me seats in homes not my own. You have brought the distant near and made a brother of the stranger.

I am uneasy at heart when I have to leave my accustomed shelter; I forget that there abides the old in the new and that there also You abide.

Through birth and death, in this world or in others, wherever You lead me, it is You, the same, the one Companion of my endless life, who links my heart with bonds of joy to the unfamiliar.

When one knows You, then alien there is none, then no door is shut. O grant me my prayer that I may never lose the bliss of the touch of the one in the play of the many.

You Hide Yourself

You hide Yourself in Your own glory, O God. The sand-grain and the dewdrop are more proudly apparent than You are.

The world unabashed calls all things his own that are Yours—yet it is never brought to shame.

You make room for us while standing aside in silence; wherefore, love lights her own lamp to seek You and comes to Your worship unbidden.

Freed at Last!

You took my hand and drew me to Your side, made me sit on the high seat before all others, till I became timid, unable to stir and walk my own way, doubting and debating at every step lest I should tread upon any thorn of their disfavor.

I am freed at last!

The blow has come, the drum of insult sounded, my seat is laid low in the dust.

My paths are open before me.

My wings are full of the desire of the sky.

I go to join the shooting stars of midnight, to plunge into the profound shadow.

I am like the storm-driven cloud of summer that, having cast off its crown of gold, hangs as a sword the thunderbolt upon a chain of lightning.

In desperate joy I run upon the dusty paths of the despised; I draw near to Your final welcome.

The child finds its mother when it leaves her womb. When I am parted from You, thrown out from Your household, I am free to see Your face.

Eternal Traveler

You will find, Eternal Traveler, marks of Your footsteps across my songs.

Yours

Yours is the light that breaks forth from the dark, and the good that sprouts from the deft heart of strife.

Yours is the house that opens upon the world, and the love that calls to the battlefield.

Yours is the gift that still is a gain when everything is a loss, and the life that flows through the caverns of death.

Yours is the heaven that lies in the common dust, and You are there for me; You are there for all.

Worship

Your gifts to us mortals fulfill all our needs and yet run back to You undiminished.

The river has its everyday work to do and hastens through the fields and hamlets; yet its incessant stream winds toward the washing of Your feet.

The flower sweetens the air with its perfume; yet its last service is to offer itself to You.

Your worship does not diminish the world.

From the words of the poet, people take what meanings please them; yet their last meaning points to You.

The Perfect Union

Your joy in me is full.

You have taken me as Your partner of all this wealth. In my heart is the endless play of Your delight. In my life, Your will is ever taking shape.

You who are the Ruler of rulers have decked Yourself in beauty, and Your love loses itself in the love of Your lover in the perfect union of two.

Your Light, My Light

Your light, my light, world-filling light, the dancing center of my life, the sky breaks forth, the wind runs wild, and laughter passes over the earth.

The butterflies have spread their sails to glide up on the seas of light; the lilies and the jasmine flowers surge on the crest of waves of light.

Now heaven's river drowns its banks, and floods of joy have run abroad; now mirth has spread from leaf to leaf, and gladness without measure comes.

Your Sunbeams

Your sunbeams come upon this earth of mine with arms outstretched and stand at my door the livelong day to carry back to Your feet clouds made of my tears and sighs and songs.

With fond delight, You wrap about Your starry breast that mantle of misty cloud, turning it into numberless shapes and folds and coloring it with hues ever changing.

It is so light and so fleeting, tender and tearful and dark, that is why You love it, O Serene One, and that is why it may cover Your awful white light with its shadows of Your suffering.

A Ray of Morning Sun

A ray of morning sun strikes aslant at the door.

The assembled crowd feel in their blood the primaeval chant of creation:

"Mother, open the gate!"

The gate opens.

The mother is seated on a straw bed with the babe on her lap,

Like the dawn with the morning star.

The sun's ray that was waiting at the door outside falls on the head of the child.

The poet strikes his lute and sings out:

"Victory to Man, the new-born, the ever-living."

They kneel down, the king and the beggar, the saint and the sinner, the wise and the fool, and cry:

"Victory to Man, the new-born, the ever-living."

The old man from the East murmurs to himself:

"I have seen!"

A Hundred Years from Now

Who are you, reader, reading my poems an hundred years hence?

I cannot send you one single flower from this wealth of the spring, one single streak of gold from yonder clouds.

Open your doors and look abroad.
From your blossoming garden gather fragrant memories of the vanished flowers of a hundred years before.

In the joy of your heart may you feel the living joy that sang one spring morning, sending its glad voice across a hundred years.